TOUR
COUTURE

AN ILLUSTRATED GUIDE TO WHAT
TAYLOR SWIFT WORE AND WHEN

Kimberly Macnider

TOUR COUTURE by Kimberly Macnider

contact@kimberlymacnider.com
kimberlymacnider.com

ISBN 979-8-9929571-0-5

oh hi!

CONTENTS

MICROPHONES

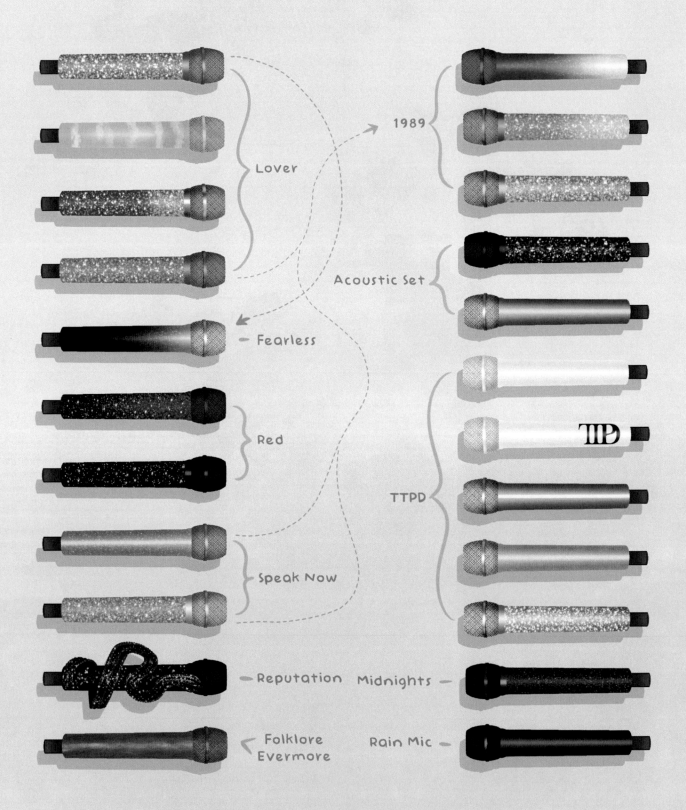

Lover

1989

Acoustic Set

Fearless

Red

TTPD

Speak Now

Reputation   Midnights

Folklore
Evermore   Rain Mic

GUITARS

Lover
Gibson J-180
"Custom"

Lover
Gibson J-180
"Custom"

Fearless
Gibson J-180
"Custom"
Designed by
Taylor Swift's
Parents

Lover
Gibson J-180
"Custom"

Red
Gibson J-45
"Custom"

Red
Gibson J-45
"Custom"

Speak Now
Taylor Grand-
Symphony
"Living Jewels"
"LE 100"

folklore
Gibson
"Hummingbird"

Acoustic Set
Taylor PS-24ce
Grand-
Auditorium
"Custom"

7

LOVER

VERSACE   LOUBOUTIN

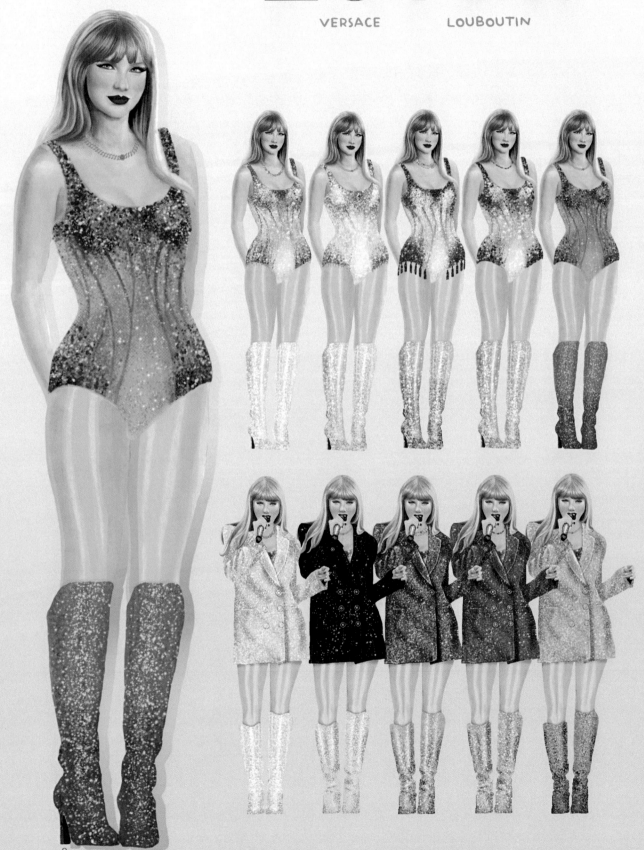

8

FEARLESS

ROBERTO CAVALLI   NAEEM KHAN   LOUBOUTIN

ROBERTO CAVALLI   ROBERTO CAVALLI   ROBERTO CAVALLI

NAEEM KHAN   ROBERTO CAVALLI   ROBERTO CAVALLI

RED

ASHISH   LOUBOUTIN

SPEAK NOW

NICOLE + FELICIA   ELIE SAAB   ZUHAIR MURAD   REEM ACRA

NICOLE + FELICIA   ZUHAIR MURAD   ELIE SAAB   ELIE SAAB

NICOLE + FELICIA   NICOLE + FELICIA   REEM ACRA   REEM ACRA

REPUTATION

ROBERTO CAVALLI

FOLKLORE

ALBERTA FERRETTI   LOUBOUTIN

EVERMORE

ETRO   ALBERTA FERRETTI   LOUBOUTIN

1989

ROBERTO CAVALLI   LOUBOUTIN

THE TORTURED POETS DEPARTMENT

VIVIENNE WESTWOOD   LOUBOUTIN

16

THE ACOUSTIC SET

JESSICA JONES   ROBERTO CAVALLI   LOUBOUTIN

17

MIDNIGHTS

OSCAR DE LA RENTA   ZUHAIR MURAD   JENNY PACKHAM   LOUBOUTIN

OSCAR DE LA RENTA   OSCAR DE LA RENTA   OSCAR DE LA RENTA   OSCAR DE LA RENTA   OSCAR DE LA RENTA   OSCAR DE LA RENTA   JENNY PACKHAM   JENNY PACKHAM

OSCAR DE LA RENTA   ZUHAIR MURAD   ZUHAIR MURAD   ZUHAIR MURAD   ZUHAIR MURAD

SETLIST

FIRST LEG

Miss Americana & The Heartbreak Prince
Cruel Summer
The Man
You Need to Calm Down
Lover
The Archer
Fearless
You Belong With Me
Love Story
'tis the damn season
(no body, no crime)
willow
marjorie
champagne problems
tolerate it
...Ready For It?
Delicate
Don't Blame Me
Look What You Made Me Do
Enchanted
(Long Live)
22
We Are Never Ever Getting Back Together
I Knew You Were Trouble
(Nothing New)
All Too Well (10 Minute Version)
(invisible string)
the 1
betty
the last great american dynasty
august
illicit affairs
my tears ricochet
cardigan
Style
Blank Space
Shake It Off
Wildest Dreams
Bad Blood
(Acoustic 1)
(Acoustic 2)
Lavender Haze
Anti-Hero
Midnight Rain
Vigilante Shit
Bejeweled
Mastermind
Karma

SECOND LEG

Miss Americana & The Heartbreak Prince
Cruel Summer
The Man
You Need to Calm Down
Lover
Fearless
You Belong With Me
Love Story
22
We Are Never Ever Getting Back Together
I Knew You Were Trouble
All Too Well (10 Minute Version)
Enchanted
...Ready For It?
Delicate
Don't Blame Me
Look What You Made Me Do
cardigan
betty
champagne problems
august
illicit affairs
my tears ricochet
marjorie
willow
Style
Blank Space
Shake It Off
Wildest Dreams
Bad Blood
But Daddy I Love Him
So High School
(Florida!!!)
Who's Afraid of Little Old Me?
Down Bad
Fortnight
The Smallest Man Who Ever Lived
I Can Do It With a Broken Heart
(Acoustic 1)
(Acoustic 2)
Lavender Haze
Anti-Hero
Midnight Rain
Vigilante Shit
Bejeweled
Mastermind
Karma

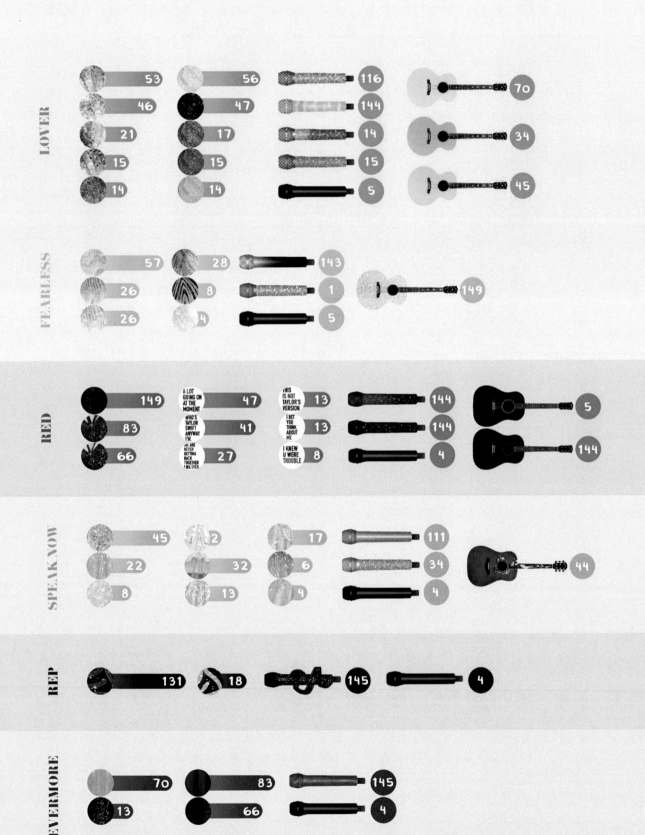

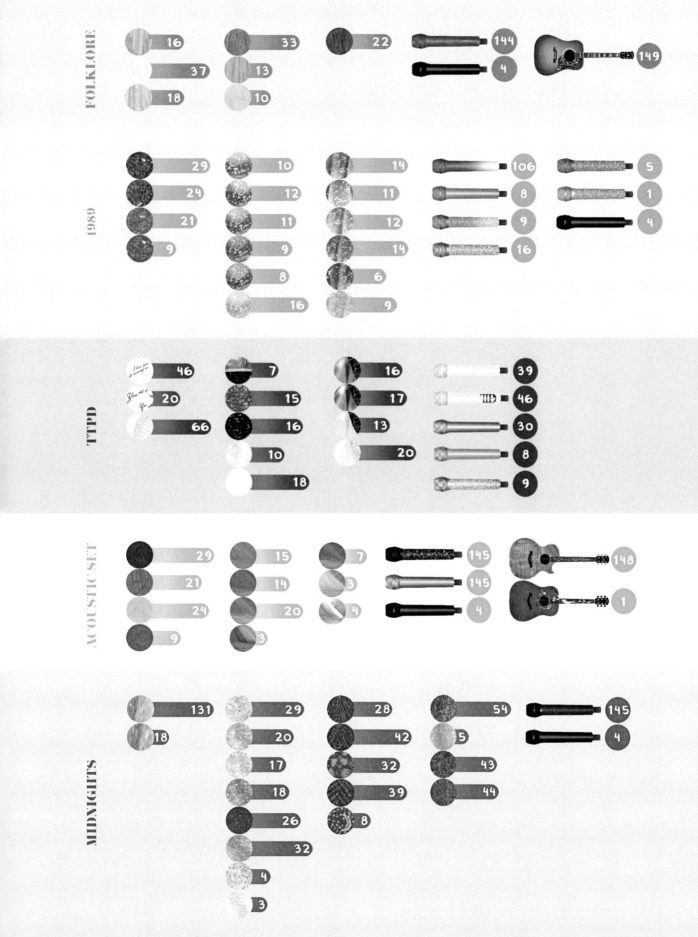

FOLKLORE

16
37
18
33
13
10
22
144
4
149

1989

29
24
21
9
10
12
11
9
8
16
14
11
12
14
6
9
106
8
9
16
5
1
4

TTPD

46
20
66
7
15
16
10
18
16
17
13
20
39
46
30
8
9

ACOUSTIC SET

29
21
24
9
15
14
20
3
7
3
4
145
145
4
148
1

MIDNIGHTS

131
18
29
20
17
18
26
32
4
3
28
42
32
39
8
54
5
43
44
145
4

21

GLENDALE, AZ

State Farm Stadium
March 17, 2023

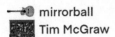 mirrorball
Tim McGraw

Opener - GAYLE / Paramore

22

GLENDALE, AZ

State Farm Stadium
March 18, 2023

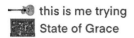 this is me trying
State of Grace

Opener - GAYLE / Paramore

23

Allegiant Stadium
March 24, 2023

Our Song
Snow On The Beach

Opener - GAYLE / beabadoobee

LAS VEGAS, NV

Allegiant Stadium
March 25, 2023

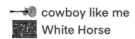 cowboy like me
White Horse

Opener - GAYLE / beabadoobee
Special Guest - Marcus Mumford

25

ARLINGTON, TX

AT&T Stadium
March 31, 2023

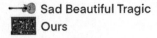 Sad Beautiful Tragic

Ours

Opener - MUNA / GAYLE

26

ARLINGTON, TX

AT&T Stadium
April 1, 2023

 Death By A Thousand Cuts
Clean

Opener - beabadoobee / Gracie Abrams

ARLINGTON, TX

AT&T Stadium
April 2, 2023

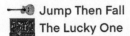 Jump Then Fall
The Lucky One

Opener - beabadoobee / Gracie Abrams

 Speak Now
Treacherous

Opener - beabadoobee / GAYLE

TAMPA, FL
Raymond James Stadium
April 14, 2023

🎸 The Great War
▦ You're On Your Own, Kid

Opener - beabadoobee / Gracie Abrams
Special Guest - Aaron Dessner

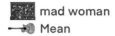 mad woman

Mean

Opener - beabadoobee / Gracie Abrams
Special Guest - Aaron Dessner

TAMPA, FL
Raymond James Stadium
April 15, 2023

31

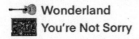 Wonderland
You're Not Sorry

Opener - beabadoobee / Gracie Abrams

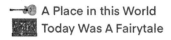 A Place in this World

Today Was A Fairytale

Opener - beabadoobee / Gracie Abrams

33

HOUSTON, TX

NRG Stadium
April 23, 2023

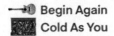 Begin Again
Cold As You

Opener - beabadoobee / Gracie Abrams

34

ATLANTA, GA

Mercedes-Benz Stadium
April 28, 2023

 The Other Side Of The Door

coney island

Opener - beabadoobee / Gracie Abrams

35

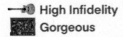 High Infidelity
Gorgeous

Opener - beabadoobee / Gracie Abrams

ATLANTA, GA
Mercedes-Benz Stadium
April 29, 2023

ATLANTA, GA

Mercedes-Benz Stadium
April 30, 2023

I Bet You Think About Me
How You Get The Girl

Opener - MUNA / GAYLE

NASHVILLE, TN

Nissan Stadium
May 5, 2023

 Sparks Fly
Teardrops On My Guitar

Opener - Phoebe Bridgers / Gracie Abrams
Special Guest - Phoebe Bridgers
Announcement - Speak Now (Taylor's Version)

NASHVILLE, TN

Nissan Stadium
May 6, 2023

Out Of The Woods
Fifteen

Opener - Phoebe Bridgers / GAYLE
Special Guest - Phoebe Bridgers

NASHVILLE, TN

Nissan Stadium
May 7, 2023

Would've, Could've, Should've
Mine

Opener - Phoebe Bridgers (Canceled) / Gracie Abrams (Canceled)
Special Guest - Phoebe Bridgers / Aaron Dessner

PHILADELPHIA, PA

Lincoln Financial Field
May 12, 2023

gold rush
Come Back...Be Here

Opener - Phoebe Bridgers / GAYLE
Special Guest - Phoebe Bridgers

PHILADELPHIA, PA

Lincoln Financial Field
May 13, 2023

 Forever & Always
This Love

Opener - Phoebe Bridgers / GAYLE
Special Guest - Phoebe Bridgers

PHILADELPHIA, PA

Lincoln Financial Field
May 14, 2023

Hey Stephen
The Best Day

Opener - Phoebe Bridgers / Gracie Abrams
Special Guest - Phoebe Bridgers

43

FOXBOROUGH, MA

Gillette Stadium
May 19, 2023

🎸 Should've Said No
Better Man

Opener - Phoebe Bridgers / GAYLE
Special Guest - Phoebe Bridgers

FOXBOROUGH, MA

Gillette Stadium
May 20, 2023

Question...?
Invisible

Opener - Phoebe Bridgers / GAYLE
Special Guest - Phoebe Bridgers

FOXBOROUGH, MA

Gillette Stadium
May 21, 2023

 I Think He Knows
Red

Opener - Phoebe Bridgers / Gracie Abrams
Special Guest - Phoebe Bridgers

46

EAST RUTHERFORD, NJ

MetLife Stadium
May 26, 2023

 Getaway Car
Maroon

Opener – Phoebe Bridgers / GAYLE
Special Guest – Phoebe Bridgers / Jack Antonoff / Ice Spice
Music Video Premiere – Karma ft. Ice Spice

EAST RUTHERFORD, NJ

 Holy Ground
False God

Opener - Phoebe Bridgers / Gracie Abrams
Special Guest - Phoebe Bridgers / Ice Spice

48

EAST RUTHERFORD, NJ

MetLife Stadium
May 28, 2023

 Welcome To New York
Clean

Opener - Phoebe Bridgers / OWENN
Special Guest - Phoebe Bridgers / Ice Spice

CHICAGO, IL

Soldier Field
June 2, 2023

 I Wish You Would
the lakes

Opener - Girl In Red / OWENN

50

You All Over Me
I Don't Wanna Live Forever

Opener - Girl In Red / OWENN
Special Guest - Maren Morris

51

CHICAGO, IL
Soldier Field
June 4, 2023

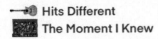 Hits Different
The Moment I Knew

Opener - MUNA / Gracie Abrams

52

DETROIT, MI

Ford Field
June 9, 2023

 Haunted
I Almost Do

Opener - Girl In Red / Gracie Abrams

DETROIT, MI

Ford Field
June 10, 2023

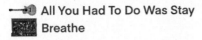 All You Had To Do Was Stay

Breathe

Opener - Girl In Red / OWENN

PITTSBURGH, PA

Acrisure Stadium
June 16, 2023

Mr. Perfectly Fine
The Last Time

Opener - Girl In Red / Gracie Abrams

PITTSBURGH, PA

Acrisure Stadium
June 17, 2023

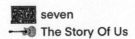 seven

The Story Of Us

Opener - Girl In Red / OWENN
Special Guest - Aaron Dessner

MINNEAPOLIS, MN

U.S. Bank Stadium
June 23, 2023

🎸 Paper Rings
🖼️ If This Was A Movie

Opener - Girl In Red / Gracie Abrams

MINNEAPOLIS, MN

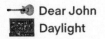 Dear John
Daylight

Opener - Girl In Red / OWENN

CINCINNATI, OH

Paycor Stadium
June 30, 2023

 I'm Only Me When I'm With You
evermore

Opener - MUNA / Gracie Abrams

CINCINNATI, OH

Paycor Stadium
July 1, 2023

 ivy

 I miss you, I'm sorry

Call It What You Want

Opener - MUNA / Gracie Abrams (canceled)

Special Guest - Aaron Dessner / Gracie Abrams

60

KANSAS CITY, MO

Never Grow Up
When Emma Falls in Love

Opener - MUNA / Gracie Abrams
Special Guest - Joey King / Presley Cash / Taylor Lautner
Music Video Premiere - I Can See You

KANSAS CITY, MO

GEHA Field at Arrowhead Stadium
July 8, 2023

 Last Kiss
dorothea

Opener - MUNA / Gracie Abrams

DENVER, CO

Empower Field at Mile High
July 14, 2023

Picture To Burn
Timeless

Opener - MUNA / Gracie Abrams

Starlight
Back To December

Opener - MUNA / Gracie Abrams

DENVER, CO
Empower Field at Mile High
July 15, 2023

SEATTLE, WA

Lumen Field
July 22, 2023

 This Is Why We Can't Have Nice Things
Everything Has Changed

Opener - HAIM / Gracie Abrams
Special Guest - HAIM

65

SEATTLE, WA
Lumen Field
July 23, 2023

 Message In A Bottle
Tied Together with a Smile

Opener - HAIM / Gracie Abrams
Special Guest - HAIM

66

SANTA CLARA, CA

Levi's Stadium
July 28, 2023

 right where you left me
Castles Crumbling

Opener - HAIM / Gracie Abrams
Special Guest - HAIM / Aaron Dessner

SANTA CLARA, CA

Levi's Stadium
July 29, 2023

Stay Stay Stay
All Of The Girls You Loved Before

Opener - HAIM / Gracie Abrams
Special Guest - HAIM

LOS ANGELES, CA

SoFi Stadium
August 3, 2023

I Can See You
Maroon

Opener - HAIM / Gracie Abrams
Special Guest - HAIM

LOS ANGELES, CA

SoFi Stadium
August 4, 2023

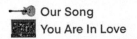

Our Song
You Are In Love

Opener - HAIM / OWENN
Special Guest - HAIM

70

LOS ANGELES, CA

 Death By A Thousand Cuts
You're On Your Own, Kid

Opener - HAIM / GAYLE
Special Guest - HAIM

71

LOS ANGELES, CA

SoFi Stadium
August 7, 2023

 Dress
exile

Opener - HAIM / Gracie Abrams
Special Guest - HAIM

72

LOS ANGELES, CA

SoFi Stadium
August 8, 2023

I Know Places
King Of My Heart

Opener - HAIM / Gracie Abrams
Special Guest - HAIM

73

LOS ANGELES, CA

SoFi Stadium
August 9, 2023

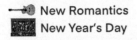
New Romantics
New Year's Day

Opener - HAIM / GAYLE
Special Guest - HAIM
Announcement - 1989 (Taylor's Version)

MEXICO CITY, MX

Foro Sol
August 24, 2023

I Forgot That You Existed
Sweet Nothing

Opener - Sabrina Carpenter

75

MEXICO CITY, MX

Foro Sol
August 25, 2023

Tell Me Why
Snow On The Beach

Opener - Sabrina Carpenter

MEXICO CITY, MX

Foro Sol
August 26, 2023

Cornelia Street
You're On Your Own, Kid

Opener - Sabrina Carpenter

MEXICO CITY, MX

Foro Sol
August 27, 2023

 Afterglow
Maroon

Opener - Sabrina Carpenter

BUENOS AIRES, AR

Estadio River Plate
November 9, 2023

The Very First Night
Labyrinth

Opener - LOUTA / Sabrina Carpenter

BUENOS AIRES, AR

Estadio River Plate
November 11, 2023

🎸 Is It Over Now? / Out Of The Woods
▦ End Game

Opener - LOUTA / Sabrina Carpenter

BUENOS AIRES, AR

Estadio River Plate
November 12, 2023

Better Than Revenge
"Slut!"

Opener - LOUTA / Sabrina Carpenter

RIO DE JANEIRO, BR

Estádio Nilton Santos
November 17, 2023

 Stay Beautiful

Suburban Legends

Opener - Sabrina Carpenter

82

RIO DE JANEIRO, BR

Estádio Nilton Santos
November 19, 2023

Dancing With Our Hands Tied
Bigger Than The Whole Sky

Opener - Sabrina Carpenter

RIO DE JANEIRO, BR

Estádio Nilton Santos
November 20, 2023

ME!
So It Goes...

Opener - Sabrina Carpenter

84

SÃO PAULO, BR

Allianz Parque
November 24, 2023

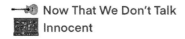
Now That We Don't Talk
Innocent

Opener - Sabrina Carpenter

SÃO PAULO, BR

Allianz Parque
November 25, 2023

 Safe & Sound
Untouchable

Opener - Sabrina Carpenter

Say Don't Go

it's time to go

Opener - Sabrina Carpenter

87

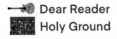

Dear Reader
Holy Ground

88

Eyes Open
Electric Touch

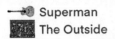

Superman
The Outside

90

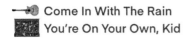
Come In With The Rain
You're On Your Own, Kid

MELBOURNE, AU

Melbourne Cricket Ground
February 16, 2024

 Red

You're Losing Me

Opener - Sabrina Carpenter
Announcement - TTPD 'The Bolter' Variant

MELBOURNE, AU

Melbourne Cricket Ground
February 17, 2024

 Getaway Car / august / The Other Side Of The Door
this is me trying

Opener - Sabrina Carpenter

MELBOURNE, AU

Melbourne Cricket Ground
February 18, 2024

Come Back...Be Here / Daylight
Teardrops On My Guitar

Opener - Sabrina Carpenter

SYDNEY, AU

Accor Stadium
February 23, 2024

 How You Get The Girl
White Horse / coney island

Opener - Sabrina Carpenter (canceled)
Special Guest - Sabrina Carpenter
Announcement - TTPD 'The Albatross' Variant

SYDNEY, AU

Accor Stadium
February 24, 2024

Should've Said No / You're Not Sorry
New Year's Day / Peace

Opener - Sabrina Carpenter

SYDNEY, AU

Accor Stadium
February 25, 2024

 Is It Over Now? / I Wish You Would

Haunted / exile

Opener - Sabrina Carpenter

SYDNEY, AU

Accor Stadium
February 26, 2024

 Would've, Could've, Should've / ivy
Forever & Always / Maroon

Opener - Sabrina Carpenter

SINGAPORE

National Stadium
March 2, 2024

 Mine / Starlight
I Don't Wanna Live Forever / Dress

Opener - Sabrina Carpenter

99

SINGAPORE
National Stadium
March 3, 2024

 long story short / The Story Of Us

Clean / evermore

Opener – Sabrina Carpenter
Announcement – TTPD 'The Black Dog' Variant

SINGAPORE

National Stadium
March 4, 2024

🎸 Foolish One / Tell Me Why
This Love / Call It What You Want

Opener - Sabrina Carpenter

SINGAPORE

National Stadium
March 7, 2024

Death By A Thousand Cuts / Babe
Fifteen / You're On Your Own, Kid

Opener - Sabrina Carpenter

102

SINGAPORE

National Stadium
March 8, 2024

Sparks Fly / gold rush
False God / "Slut!"

Opener - Sabrina Carpenter

SINGAPORE

National Stadium
March 9, 2024

 Tim McGraw / cowboy like me
mirrorball / epiphany

Opener - Sabrina Carpenter

PARIS, FR

La Défense Arena
May 9, 2024

 Paris
loml

Opener - Paramore

Is It Over Now? / Out Of The Woods

My Boy Only Breaks His Favorite Toys

Opener - Paramore

Hey Stephen
Maroon

Opener - Paramore

PARIS, FR

La Défense Arena
May 11, 2024

PARIS, FR
La Défense Arena
May 12, 2024

The Alchemy / Treacherous

Begin Again / Paris

Opener - Paramore

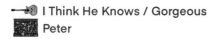 I Think He Knows / Gorgeous

Peter

Opener - Paramore

STOCKHOLM, SE

Friends Arena
May 18, 2024

🎤 Guilty as Sin?
▪️ Say Don't Go / Welcome To New York / Clean

Opener - Paramore

110

STOCKHOLM, SE

 Message In A Bottle / How You Get The Girl / New Romantics
How Did It End?

Opener - Paramore

🎸 Come Back...Be Here / The Way I Loved You / The Other Side Of The Door

 Fresh Out The Slammer / High Infidelity

Opener - Paramore

112

Estádio da Luz
May 25, 2024

The Tortured Poets Department /
Now That We Don't Talk

You're On Your Own, Kid / Long Live

Opener - Paramore

MADRID, ES

Estadio Santiago Bernabéu
May 29, 2024

 Sparks Fly / I Can Fix Him (No Really I Can)
I Look in People's Windows / Snow On The Beach

Opener - Paramore

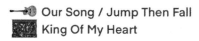
Our Song / Jump Then Fall
King Of My Heart

Opener - Paramore

MADRID, ES
Estadio Santiago Bernabéu
May 30, 2024

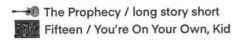

The Prophecy / long story short
Fifteen / You're On Your Own, Kid

Opener - Paramore

LYON, FR
Groupama Stadium
June 2, 2024

116

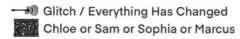 Glitch / Everything Has Changed

Chloe or Sam or Sophia or Marcus

Opener - Paramore

117

EDINBURGH, UK

Scottish Gas Murrayfield Stadium
June 7, 2024

Would've, Could've, Should've / I Know Places
'tis the damn season / Daylight

Opener - Paramore

EDINBURGH, UK

Scottish Gas Murrayfield Stadium
June 8, 2024

 The Bolter / Getaway Car

 All Of The Girls You Loved Before / Crazier

Opener - Paramore

119

EDINBURGH, UK

Scottish Gas Murrayfield Stadium
June 9, 2024

 It's Nice To Have A Friend / Dorothea

Haunted / exile

Opener - Paramore

120

LIVERPOOL, UK

Anfield
June 13, 2024

I Can See You / Mine

Cornelia Street/ Maroon

Opener - Paramore

LIVERPOOL, UK

Anfield
June 14, 2024

 This Is What You Came For / gold rush
The Great War / You're Losing Me

Opener - Paramore

122

LIVERPOOL, UK
Anfield
June 15, 2024

 Carolina / no body, no crime

The Manuscript / Red

Opener - Paramore

123

CARDIFF, UK

Principality Stadium
June 18, 2024

 I Forgot That You Existed /
This Is Why We Can't Have Nice Things

I Hate It Here / the lakes

Opener - Paramore

124

LONDON, UK

Wembley Stadium
June 21, 2024

 Hits Different / Death By A Thousand Cuts
The Black Dog / Come Back...Be Here / Maroon

Opener - METTE / Paramore

125

LONDON, UK

Wembley Stadium
June 22, 2024

 thanK you aIMee / Mean
Castles Crumbling

Opener - Griff / Paramore
Special Guest - Hayley Williams

126

LONDON, UK

Wembley Stadium
June 23, 2024

 Us
Out Of The Woods / Is It Over Now? / Clean

Opener - Benson Boone / Paramore
Special Guest - Travis Kelce / Gracie Abrams

127

State Of Grace / You're On Your Own, Kid
Sweet Nothing / hoax

Opener - Paramore

DUBLIN, IE

Aviva Stadium
June 29, 2024

The Albatross / Dancing With Our Hands Tied
This Love / Ours

Opener - Paramore

DUBLIN, IE

Aviva Stadium
June 30, 2024

Clara Bow / The Lucky One
You're On You're Own, Kid

Opener - Paramore

AMSTERDAM, NL

Johan Cruijff Arena
July 4, 2024

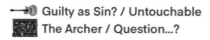
Guilty as Sin? / Untouchable
The Archer / Question...?

Opener - Paramore

131

AMSTERDAM, NL

Johan Cruijff Arena
July 5, 2024

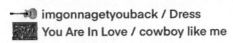 imgonnagetyouback / Dress
You Are In Love / cowboy like me

Opener - Paramore

AMSTERDAM, NL

Johan Cruijff Arena
July 6, 2024

 Sweeter Than Fiction / Holy Ground
Mary's Song (Oh My My My) / So High School /
Everything Has Changed

Opener - Paramore

133

ZÜRICH, CH
Stadion Letzigrund
July 9, 2024

🎸 right where you left me /
   All You Had To Do Was Stay
▓▓ Last Kiss / Sad Beautiful Tragic

Opener - Paramore

134

ZÜRICH, CH

closure / A Perfectly Good Heart
Robin / Never Grow Up

Opener - Paramore

135

MILAN, IT

San Siro Stadium
July 13, 2024

the 1 / Wonderland
I Almost Do / The Moment I Knew

Opener - Paramore

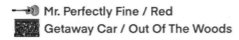 Mr. Perfectly Fine / Red

Getaway Car / Out Of The Woods

Opener - Paramore

GELSENKIRCHEN, DE

VELTINS-Arena
July 17, 2024

 Superstar / invisible string

"Slut!" / False God

Opener - Paramore

GELSENKIRCHEN, DE

Speak Now / Hey Stephen

this is me trying / Labyrinth

Opener - Paramore

GELSENKIRCHEN, DE

VELTINS-Arena
July 19, 2024

🎤 Paper Rings / Stay Stay Stay
📦 it's time to go / Better Man

Opener - Paramore

140

HAMBURG, DE

Volksparkstadion
July 23, 2024

Teardrops On My Guitar / The Last Time
We Were Happy / happiness

Opener - Paramore

HAMBURG, DE
Volksparkstadion
July 24, 2024

 the last great american dynasty / Run
Nothing New / Dear Reader

Opener - Paramore

142

MUNICH, DE

Olympiastadion
July 27, 2024

 Fresh Out The Slammer / You Are In Love
ivy / Call It What You Want

Opener - Paramore

I Don't Wanna Live Forever / imgonnagetyouback
loml / Don't You

Opener - Paramore

WARSAW, PL

PGE Narodowy
August 1, 2024

mirrorball / Clara Bow
Suburban Legends / New Year's Day

Opener - Paramore

145

I Can Fix Him (No Really I Can) / I Can See You
Red / Maroon

Opener - Paramore

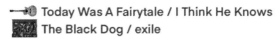 Today Was A Fairytale / I Think He Knows

The Black Dog / exile

Opener - Paramore

August 8   August 9   August 10

LONDON, UK

Wembley Stadium
August 15, 2024

 Everything Has Changed / End Game / Thinking Out Loud

King Of My Heart / The Alchemy

Opener - SOFIA ISELLA / Paramore
Special Guest - Ed Sheeran

LONDON, UK

Wembley Stadium
August 16, 2024

 London Boy

Dear John / Sad Beautiful Tragic

Opener - Holly Humberstone / Paramore

LONDON, UK

Wembley Stadium
August 17, 2024

 I Did Something Bad
My Boy Only Breaks His Favorite Toys /
coney island

Opener - Suki Waterhouse / Paramore

151

LONDON, UK

Wembley Stadium
August 19, 2024

Long Live / Change

The Archer / You're On You're Own, Kid

Opener - Maisie Peters / Paramore

LONDON, UK
Wembley Stadium
August 20, 2024

 Death By A Thousand Cuts / Getaway Car
So Long, London

Opener - RAYE / Paramore
Special Guest - Florence Welch / Jack Antonoff
Music Video Premiere - "I Can Do It With A Broken Heart"

153

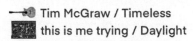
Tim McGraw / Timeless
this is me trying / Daylight

Opener - Gracie Abrams
Special Guest - Florence Welch

154

Should've Said No / I Did Something Bad
loml / White Horse

Opener - Gracie Abrams
Special Guest - Florence Welch

🎸 Out Of The Woods / All You Had To Do Was Stay
🎹 mirrorball / Guilty as Sin?

Opener - Gracie Abrams
Special Guest - Florence Welch

156

NEW ORLEANS, LO

 Our Song / Call It What You Want
The Black Dog / Haunted

Opener - Gracie Abrams

157

NEW ORLEANS, LO

Caesars Superdome
October 26, 2024

Espresso / Is It Over Now? / Please Please Please

Hits Different / Welcome To New York

Opener - Gracie Abrams
Special Guest - Sabrina Carpenter

NEW ORLEANS, LO

Afterglow / Dress
How You Get The Girl / Clean

Opener - Gracie Abrams

INDIANAPOLIS, IN

Lucas Oil Stadium
November 1, 2024

 The Albatross / Holy Ground
Cold As You / exile

Opener - Gracie Abrams

160

INDIANAPOLIS, IN

Lucas Oil Stadium
November 2, 2024

 The Prophecy / This Love
Maroon / cowboy like me

Opener - Gracie Abrams

INDIANAPOLIS, IN

Lucas Oil Stadium
November 3, 2024

🎸 Cornelia Street / The Bolter
🔊 Death By A Thousand Cuts / The Great War

Opener - Gracie Abrams

TORONTO, ON

Rogers Centre
November 14, 2024

🎸 My Boy Only Breaks His Favorite Toys /
This Is Why We Can't Have Nice Things
▨ False God / 'tis the damn season

Opener - Gracie Abrams

163

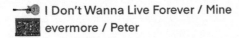

I Don't Wanna Live Forever / Mine

evermore / Peter

Opener - Gracie Abrams

164

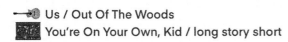
Us / Out Of The Woods
You're On Your Own, Kid / long story short

Opener - Gracie Abrams
Special Guest - Gracie Abrams

165

Mr. Perfectly Fine / Better Than Revenge
State Of Grace / Labyrinth

Opener - Gracie Abrams

166

TORONTO, ON

Rogers Centre
November 22, 2024

Ours / the last great american dynasty
Cassandra / mad woman / I Did Something Bad

Opener - Gracie Abrams

167

TORONTO, ON

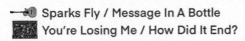 Sparks Fly / Message In A Bottle

You're Losing Me / How Did It End?

Opener - Gracie Abrams

168

VANCOUVER, BC

 Haunted / Wonderland
Never Grow Up / The Best Day

Opener - Gracie Abrams

VANCOUVER, BC

BC Place
December 7, 2024

 I Love You, I'm Sorry / Last Kiss
The Tortured Poets Department / Maroon

Opener - Gracie Abrams
Special Guest - Gracie Abrams

VANCOUVER, BC

BC Place
December 8, 2024

A Place in this World / New Romantics
Long Live / New Year's Day / The Manuscript

Opener - Gracie Abrams

TAYLOR SWIFT THE ERAS TOUR

In Theater
October 13, 2023

Our Song
You're On Your Own, Kid

Credits - Long Live

172

Thank you to Taylor Swift. The Eras Tour was a masterpiece, and I'm beyond grateful to have experienced this phenomenal piece of art and history. Your passion, creativity, and unbelievable work ethic made The Eras Tour so much bigger than just a tour. We have been forever changed.

Thank you to all the Swifties who shared their memories online, making this book possible. I have watched thousands upon thousands of videos trying to get all the details just right. It was a privilege to share in some of your happiest moments. I cried right alongside you.

"So make the friendship bracelets,
take the moment and taste it."

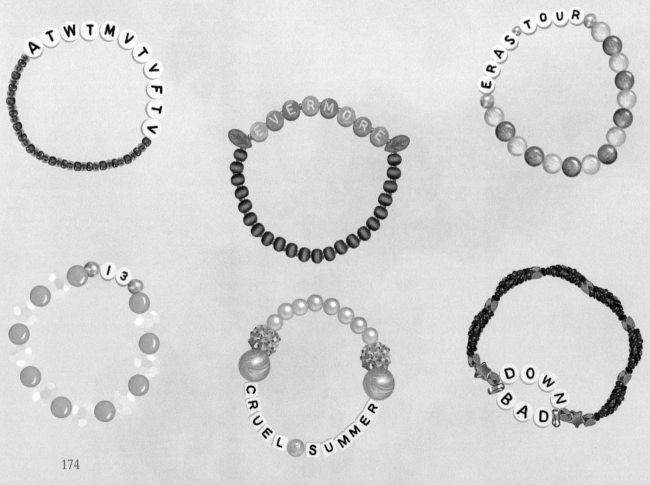

174

f75a4ac1-dbfe-4559-9067-d831a761fc37R01